THE ORIGIN

Nakayama, Kunitaka

© 2011 Nakayama, Kunitaka. All rights reserved.

ISBN978-1-257-80565-5

THE ORIGIN
CONTENTS

Preface 5

PART I. Love & Intellect
1) Money 7
2) Central Government and Central Bank........................11
3) Money-lending..16
4) Inflation 24
5) Deflation..25

PART II. Justice & Love
6) Justice and Love...31
7) Encouragement 35
8) Summary...37

PART III. Practise in Nepal
9) Nepal..40
10) The Project in Khalchet village,
    Sangkosh, Dhading, Nepal 41
11) Policy Proposal For The Nepali Government...................44
12) Foreign Currency 48

Epilogue 50

Preface

I made up my mind to be a politician when I was fifteen years old. I had already been very fond of delving into philosophical truths by the time and I read Plato's books at the age of eighteen.
It was a big intellectual and spiritual amazement, amusement, too, to me to read how Socrates and Plato pursued their philosophical research in their lives, and since then Plato became a guiding star of my philosophical and political quest for truths, and his masterpiece "Republic" became my bible.

"The philosophers must become kings in our cities," I (Socrates) said, "or those who are now called kings and potentates must learn to seek wisdom like true and genuine philosophers, and so political power and intellectual wisdom will be joined in one; and the crowds of natures who now pursue one or the other separately must be educated. Until that happens, my dear Glaucon, there can be no rest from troubles for the cities, and I think for the whole human race. Until then, this constitution which we have now evolved in works will never grow into being, as something possible; it will never see the light of the sun, but it will live only in our description."
("Republic" Book V 473D of "Great Dialogues of Plato" translated by W.H.D. Rouse)

This is perhaps the most famous idea of Plato's known as "philosopher king" that philosopher must become politician or politician should master philosophy.
I simply without much consideration and sincerely with a deep agreement took this idea as my own motive to pursue throughout

my life when I read this part of "Republic" for the first time when I was eighteen.

This short book or essay is an achievement of my philosophical quest which has always been inspired and led by Plato's philosophy since that time. (But perhaps I have been led by Socrates as well which is my utmost pleasure if so, as we never can tell which quote is Plato's and which one is Socrates', for Plato never appears in his dialogues and makes his Guru Socrates the sole interlocutor of the superb philosophies.)

PART I. Love & Intellect

1) Money

It has been my wonder and quite a big astonishment that almost none of the theories of economics has ever defined "what money is".

There has been many a thousands of theories about how to manage economy of a nation, how to get out of recession, how to control currency rate, macro-economics, micro-economics and the policies derived from them, etc., etc.

All these arguments, theories and policies are different to one another and might have some truths in them, I hope.

However, I should like to point one ultimate pitfall or defect common to all of the theories of economics as I have just mentioned above since the time of Adam Smith, father of economics, or even since the time of Plato who also mentions economy with regards to usury (money-lender).

And if you never know the nature of money, how can you define what economy is, how economy should be managed?

But to my amazement and wonder, it seems to me that this has been the very attitude of all the economists so far.

So, as a philosopher by inclination, I have always tried to find out "what money is" in my philosophical quest and here is the answer which I have found by myself.

To begin with, let us imagine a very small village, such a simple one as we can imagine that could appear in the beginning of the history to find out how money was invented and introduced in the history of mankind.

The population of the village is, let's say, one hundred people.
The dwellers of the village are living in a happy state every day without any problem.
Do we suppose that this small village needs money?
No.
The villagers are enjoying their lives doing their primitive works and can do without money, and economy is run by barter trade.
So, let us increase the population and see what happens in the village.
Up to one hundred and twenty.
Still no need for money, I should say.
What about 200? 400?
I started a project with a native partner to develop rural villages of a local prefect of Nepal last year (2010) and the population of one of the villages is about four hundred.
It looks that they don't depend on money as much as we (developed countries) do.
So, I can fairly claim that in the village of less than five hundred people human can still manage everyday life without money. And perhaps there comes in the necessity of money when the population of a village surpasses more than five, six or seven hundred people.
What happens when the population surpasses a certain limit is that they have to evaluate the value of each goods which every villager produces for sale and start pricing the goods to sell in the market which would, we can imagine, naturally appear in such a situation. This was not required when the population was one hundred, for everyone of the village was quite well acquainted with everybody else and they knew what neighbour produces. Moreover, the economy was run based on barter trade.

But when the population has increased up to the size in which each villager can't grasp what others do in the far side of the village, and therefore such a situation caused the necessity of money to get out of the primitive production stage (in which every commodity reminds of each producer's face) to upgrade to a higher and larger level of economy (in which nobody can know who the producer of each goods is).

And in our quest the population figure is not much of importance, whether it is one hundred twenty or seven hundred.

What we have to pay our attention most is that the necessity for money comes into being as the population increases and presumably barter trade ends in accordance with the increase of the population (or the beginning of mass production).

Because nobody of the village can grasp who produces which goods.

Therefore, here we can fairly conclude one important point.

"Money comes into being when population increases."

And what if the population never changes or even decreases from one hundred?

We can also conclude that the necessity for money never comes into being, had the village continued to exist in the state of barter trade without seeing its population increase.

Then, what is the cause of increase of population?

A universally agreed answer would be that "love" causes increase of population.

And increase of population causes the necessity for money and we can imagine without any difficulty that actually it did happen in the course of history to get out of the primitive state of barter trade.

Then, can we not assert that money was invented or generated out of population increase caused by love to a large extent?

Or **in short love caused the necessity for money.**
And love in itself is something that has an intrinsic nature to grow and increase everlastingly throughout the history.
So, wherever there is love, sooner or later money must come into being at some point in the course of human history.
Therefore, love is a quintessence required for the invention of money.
Money, of course, is not love in itself, but apparently starts to appear and circulate in the village when love grows in the village and that causes the end of barter trade economy, and therefore it is quite similar to "materialisation of love" to a certain degree on this earthly world that was invented to solve the necessity of developing the commercial system and for the mankind to climb up the ladder of inevitable course of civilization as a whole which we have witnessed by ourselves in the entire history for over some thousands of years.
We can fairly conclude that this is one intrinsic nature of money.

When the village starts to get out of the barter trade, the village has gone up to a higher level of economy where it has to start mass production of any goods by which the villagers have to fulfill their increasing demands of every day life.
In order to start mass production they have to inevitably introduce division of labour which fosters specialization of jobs and accumulation of knowledge of each labour and thus making each job more and more minute and professional through the process.
This is the very process in which knowledge increases in every day work and profession along with growth of love in the village.
Therefore, it is quite natural that love and knowledge (and intellect) increase simultaneously.

In short love never grows alone without knowledge.

Love without intellect is only that of animal (even many species of animal do have intellects). Without intellect and knowledge we can't live happily as human being.

Therefore, intellect increases simultaneously when love of the village grows to start mass production and start taking the course of development of commerce, thus it is also a matter of course that money was invented by human intellect that increases along with growth of love.

Moreover, money itself is a fruit of human intellect.

So, again **we can fairly conclude that money was invented by intellect when love grows and this is another intrinsic nature of money which can be described as;**

"Money is materialization of human intellect and knowledge".

Therefore, in other words, money comes into being when love and intellect grow simultaneously.

And the more love and intellect grow, the more the population increases and the more acutely the demand for money is felt.

Therefore, **money is crystalisation of love and intellect.**

Now we can fairly claim that we have found out the moment of invention of money and the very nature of money as well.

Without understanding the nature of money, we can't grasp how to manage economy of a nation, how to get out of recession, etc., etc. which themes are too oftentimes argued without understanding the very nature of money.

2) Central Government and Central Bank

What we have to consider next is how the money was distributed in the beginning of the history.

So, let us go back to the village of one hundred people or five hundred when the money was first invented in the examination above.

In a small village like the one we are studying we can assume that there is not so much discrimination or social class as we see in our modern world.

When money was first invented and introduced to foster the trade among the villagers, we can judge that money was simply treated as a tool for circulating the goods produced in the village.

And in the village where there is no discrimination, we can easily guess how money was distributed among the villagers.

Perhaps a leader of the village who might be the oldest declared like this;

"We have just invented a very useful tool for trade of the goods! I will allocate money equally among all the villagers. Let us use it wisely."

This might be the first and most probable declaration about the use of money in the village we are now developing.

And this is how the money was first distributed amongst the villagers.

I will repeat;

Money was distributed among the villagers, and allocated and given to each one of the villagers hand to hand by the old leader of the village because they needed money for daily use, when love and intellect started to grow and increase in the village.

And this is how money was given to each one of our ancestors.

I must repeat that money was "given" and "allocated" by the leader of the village in the beginning of the history and this is how money should be allocated and "given" by the person in charge of

governing the community to each one of the community who is in need of money. This is the beginning of the circulation of money.
Perhaps it is also quite probable that in some villages leaders did not treat their villagers equally but instead they allocated money according to the size of family, industriousness, intelligence, assignment of labour, etc., etc. thus varying the amount they distributed to each one of the villagers.
However, **one very important rule must have been common to all the villages that introduced money, which is to "give" and "allocate" money to each one of the villagers when they first introduced money and this was the only method to provide villagers with money in the beginning of the history of money.**

How about borrowing and lending?
The deeds of borrowing and lending come after the allocation of money.
We can fairly judge that some one of the village was in trouble for some kind of reason and he needed more money than he was given, and he had to borrow money from someone.
So, again the first allocation of money at the very beginning stage took the form of "giving" from the leader of the village, but never borrowing or lending it from the provider of money.
Therefore, we can fairly conclude that money should be given and allocated to each one of the community (nation) by the leader of the community.
According to what standard money should be allocated is another question.
What we have to focus at the moment is how the money was distributed among the villagers in the beginning of the history and

it took the form of "giving".

Because I believe there lies a big pitfall in all the theses of economics or actual policies regarding the distribution and circulation of money, which is a crucial factor of stimulating and controlling economy, I should like to emphasize and repeat;

Money should be given by the central government (the leader of the village is president or prime minister in the modern nation) to each one of citizens of every country when love and intellect grow and increase in the nation.

This is the very method how money should be distributed in the first stage and we can imagine and conclude that it could actually happen in the beginning of the history.

Let us keep on studying how and when the leader of our village allocates money.

Money is to be introduced when love and knowledge grow in the village.

So, this is the ultimate rule concerning when money is to be minted or printed more.

Money should be printed or minted when the population grows in the village, otherwise the demand for money will surpass the supply of money and the village inevitably has to go back to barter trade economy.

And exactly when is more money to be printed?

It is, I suppose, when the village of five hundred introduced money, the leader of the village allocated money to each one of the villagers according to some standard (which is not of importance at the moment), and he must have judged that more money should be printed additionally when a baby was born in the village who is number five hundred and first villager. And then five hundred and second villager was born in the village he must have ordered the person in charge of printing (or minting) to print an additional quantity of money for the five hundred and second.

Babies can't spend money, so actually their parents must have been given the money which they needed to raise their babies.

But the ultimate rule remains the same that when the population grows, more money should be printed.

And who is the decision maker regarding when and how much money should be printed?

It should be the leader of the village, but never the person in charge of printing money.

If the person in charge of printing or minting money prints money at his own liberty without consent of the leader, there might be a possibility that he could print more money than required and he would have degraded the village economy into a chaotic state.

So, the one who has to make a decision when and how much money should be printed is the leader of the village and never the person in charge of printing or minting money.

Reinterpreting it in the modern nation, the printing of money should be controlled by the president or prime minister (or the central government) of a nation and the central bank has only to follow his decision, and the central bank is not in charge of controlling the quantity and amount of money that circulates in the nation.

In our modern world developed nations have established a totally different system of controlling the mount of money that is to circulate in the nation.

Central bank has got a super prerogative to control the money of the nation and central government is only asserting their opinions on the monetary policy, and because the central government is not given of any right to control money, central government tends to blame central bank's inability or mismanagement of the nation's economy when the economy is not running well.

However, as we have just examined, the amount and quantity of the money that is to circulate in a nation should be solely controlled by the leader of the nation or the central government (in our modern world), and the central bank in charge of printing or minting money is to follow the government's decision.

If we keep on allowing the central bank to control the quantity of the money to circulate and be accumulated in the nation, the world's economy will never get out of the chaotic state as we have seen up until now.

Central bank at best may present their opinion or advice to the leader or the government of the nation concerning the management of the economy and the entire quantity of money that circulates in the nation.

(In this book I use the word "circulate" as meaning the total sum of the quantity of the money in the nation that is both circulating in the market everyday and saved in any house of the village of the nation.)

Therefore, we can fairly conclude that the leader of a nation and the central government must be solely in charge of controlling the quantity of the money that circulates in the nation.

3) Money-lending

What we have to examine next is the deed of lending money and its perish which is very likely to happen in the near foreseeable future.

I suppose there are many people believing that lending money is one of the means to increase wealth or the amount of money to circulate or flow in the country.

However, it is quite easy to tell that such an idea is entirely wrong when it comes to a nation. Its idea is only applicable and does function in a private business.

Because the only means to increase the quantity of money is to print or mint money. (Being a non native English speaker, I am almost ignoring the terminology, usage and minute differences between "printing" and "minting", "money", "coin" and "currency". Moreover these accurate definitions are not required in this philosophical quest.)

Money is something which some one produces or manufactures by hand or machine, and money never produces money by itself.

This is so extremely a simple fact that anybody can accept.

Yet many people do fall into a false belief without consideration that lending money creates wealth somehow. Interest to be paid upon borrowing should be acquired somehow and from somewhere without printing money but the entire quantity of money never increases no matter how much money is exchanged for lending or borrowing, if the central bank never prints additional money.

(Again I am using the word "wealth" as meaning money. I know that "wealth" has something more than money, but let us just keep on ignoring a minute difference for such a definition is not required in this philosophy.)

Then, what is the nature of the deed of lending money?

Well, let us go back to our village of one hundred (or five hundred).

We have examined that the village starts to invent and use money when the village can not manage its economy by barter trade because of the increase of population.

The money is to be distributed and "given" to each one of the villagers by the leader of the village but never by the person in charge of minting it.

And when does the leader of the village decide to print an additional quantity of money?

That is when a new born baby has joined the village because increase of population is the main motive and cause for the village to move towards monetary economy.

And we have agreed that this was the probable course of history that happened.

In a small village of five hundred, seven hundred, one thousand it is not hard to grasp when and how many babies are born in the village.

However, we can imagine that it would become increasingly difficult to grasp the exact figure of the village as population increases (when the village grows into a bigger size so as to make the villagers unable to grasp its exact figure in a moment, it is no longer a village, but it is better to be called city, or the beginning of a nation, though there is no clear definition of how big a nation should be).

But if the leader of the village (or a nation) fails to supply the quantity of money that is required for the new born babies, the economy of the village would be affected badly. And yet the parents of the babies are definitely in need of money to raise their babies.

Perhaps in such a case the most probable situation we can imagine is that some one of the wealthy neighbourers would offer the parents to use his money temporarily until the leader of the village grasps the exact number of the new born babies and orders to print the additional amount of money.

Now we have found out how and when the deed of money-lending was generated in the course of human history.

So, what we have just examined is that money-lending and money-lender is generated when the leader of the village (or the nation) can not grasp the figure of the village, especially its increase and decrease of the population of the village, and the money-lender is acting as supplier of money on behalf of the leader of the village (and the person in charge of printing money) until the additionally required amount of money is printed and supplied by the leader.

Therefore, we can conclude that money-lender and the deed of money-lending were generated out of the time lag, time difference between the moment when the babies are born in the village and the time when the leader of the village correctly grasps the number of the new born babies (and the recently dead) and decides the amount of money to be printed additionally.

But if the technology was there to grasp the exact figure of the nation in a moment at anytime, we can fairly claim that there is no time lag that tolerates any one to make money by lending money.

In other words, **it is lack of the technology that can gather the statistical figure of the village in an instant, which generates, tolerates or allows money-lenders to come into being.**

Therefore, it is also fair to conclude that when the technology in the field of statistics improves and the leaders of nations can grasp the statistical figures of their nations correctly at the speed of light for instance, it is quite reasonable that the very ground which spawned the deed of money-lending and money-lenders will perish in a moment from this earthly world.

Actually we are facing such a situation in our modern world in which internet technology (information technology) has been dramatically improved.

And improvement of IT naturally fosters and leads to the advancement of statistical technology as well and it is also quite logical and natural that the improvement of IT and statistical technology will wipe out the environment in which money-lending and money-lenders can survive.

Nobody can stop this rapid advancement of IT and it is only a matter of time that IT will spread out to every village, every house, every corner of the world, which inevitably forces bankers to give up lending money and change their business.

In Japan the upper limit of the interest rate which the law permits bankers and any money lenders to take has recently sharply fallen from 29.5% down to 20%. In Korea the upper limit has also dramatically fallen. The market of money lending has been shrinking in Japan and the number of money lenders has sharply fallen over the last decade.

Therefore, internet technology will indeed wipe out money-lenders, and all the banks of the world will transform from money-lenders to pure money-investors in the very near future.

Investment alone will survive as the only means for the bankers to supply money, and this is an inevitable course of human history when we consider the nature of money and that of the deed of money-lending.

However, some might ask a question;
"What happens if the governments and central banks of the nations never give up the monetary policy based on controlling interest, even after information technology and statistics technology has reached the level where they can grasp their nations

figure (population growth and decrease) in an instant?"
The question is quite logical because perish of the very ground which spawned the deed of money lending may not lead automatically to the governments' decision to end their current monetary policy.
I should answer to such a question that if the governments never give up the current financial policy, what we will face might be a revolutionary attack by the poor people upon the rich people and their riotous abandonment of labours and services to the rich people.
As the world population has been growing, the competition to get money for survival will be keener and keener, if the central governments never supply enough money by printing money, all the nations' economy will face an ever growing demand for money and even be in danger of going back to the state of barter trade. And it will become very vividly and miserably apparent that nations will be divided into two parts; haves and not-haves of money.
And if central governments never print money and keep controlling money tight (it is happening slowly world wide now), the population of not-haves will overwhelm haves and once some leaders of not haves stand up to fight against haves, an all-out revolution will assault haves. But this situation has already been happening in developing nations but the time for such a revolution is approaching even in developed countries.
One of the examples can be found in Japan where the drastic change of government took place in 2009. The true nature of the change is that the former ruling party had been representing only the rich people for many decades since after the war and the not-haves had been neglected in the politics and they stood up to change such a situation but Japan is facing an overall deflation and

the population growth (demand for money) has already ceased, the central bank can't print more money, so, there has not occurred any situation that people rush and compete to usurp money.

But if the population were growing, Japan must have faced a serious competition to get money which could be more fierce than what is happening now, because the central bank never supplies money to the economy by printing it.

So, what we will face in the near future is a quiet revolution to stop controlling interest rate and to start investment-based management of the economy, as the country has been improving its technology concerning statistics and this improvement of technology will inevitably urge the then central government and central bank to stop the current monetary policy for sure, otherwise even the quiet Japanese people will be angry against the then government in the future.

Or there might be a compromise that banks will lend money at a rate equal to annual population growth rate of the nation, because money lenders originally appeared to replace the role of the central bank which is to supply money in accordance with growth of population.

So, interest rate should be the same as the growth rate of population at best, if allowed. But considering the nature of usury, bankers or anyone who likes to make money by lending money, they will not be satisfied with such a low rate of interest. So, they might have to change their business.

But business in itself, imagine the village of one hundred, is merely to reap what you sow, and in the village where the information of everybody runs through the village in an instant you can't produce more than required and nobody buys more than necessary, you

can't cheat anybody as everybody knows everybody else.
Therefore the "business" in the modern sense, which tends to mean to get more than you need, will also perish under the environment where the information technology will have spread throughout the world as everybody knows who is doing what on the internet. So, we can udnerstand now clearly that modern "business" only spawned out of the age where information delivery is slow and imperfect.
And this conclusion is only a reflection of the fact that business is backed up by money-lenders. Therefore, once the deed of money lending perishes, so will business. And because business, always tending to make haste to get more money, has been a big leading cause which has caused imbalance of the world economy (bubble economy and recession) and such a big cause of bubble and recession will end soon, the world economy will be very sound and moderate and free of recession and bubble but only grow steadily. In fact imperfect and slow delivery of information intertwined with growing population also provided the environment for the various kinds of evils to spawn on the earth as anybody who wishes to be negligent can escape from obligation and responsibility of daily labour by hiding himself at the back of the multitude but perfect and speedy delivery of information will wipe out such an environment in which evil or devil may creep in, as such an environment where everybody knows everybody functions better than the police.

Therefore, the monetary policy based on control of interest rate will also be nullified accordingly, for interest itself will perish soon.

4) Inflation

Inflation is a state of economy where demand surpasses supply and supply can not fulfill demand.

Then, what is the origin and cause of demand?

That is desire of human being to live in this earthly world.

This desire causes man to want many things required for survival.

When man is matured, he gets married and husband and wife need many things for their happiness, survival and children.

And what is the cause of marriage?

Love.

And what is the cause of birth of children?

That is also love.

So, everybody is born out of love of his parents and growth of population is also caused by increase of love and thus population growth also increases demand.

Therefore, we can conclude that love is the ultimate cause of demand on the earth.

We can reinterpret it as "inflation is a state of economy where demand which is caused by increase of love surpasses supply".

And love in this case is the love for others.

But do we not love ourselves as well?

Therefore, we can accurately define that love has two kinds.

One is for oneself. The other one is for others.

And both kinds of love cause desire to live and they are the ultimate causes of demand.

However, when one dies without spouse and offspring, his demand remains within the range of only his demand. He can be a Buddha with so much love for others, but in order to simplify the theory, let us ignore such kinds of exceptions. And we can not allow such an exceptional case happens all over the world, had it happened so frequently, there will be decrease of demand and population, and humankind perishes quickly.

Then, we can claim that love for others creates more demand than does the love for oneself alone.

Therefore, we must restate that love both for oneself and others create demand, but love for others creates more demand.

And when we imagine our small village of one hundred (or five hundreds, if you like), it is easy to guess when inflation is caused.

That is when love for others is growing in the village and new born babies are increasing and parents are in a happy panic to produce any kinds of goods to fulfill their babies' daily growing demand.

This is the moment when demand surpasses supply and the moment when inflation is caused in the village.

So, **we can fairly conclude that inflation is the state that love for others (cause of demand) is growing faster than the increase of supply in the village (or in a nation).**

What we need is to upgrade economics with philosophical illumination.

5) Deflation

Deflation is a phenomenon in which price of goods goes down because of over supply or of lack of demand.

Again we are going to delve this phenomenon philosophically.

Price of goods goes down, it appears, because of the invisible pressure from outside which comes from lack of demand.

So, the manufacturer has to survive by cutting the price of goods somehow. This happens particularly under recession and this is an easy case to imagine.

However, manufacturer tries to reduce the price of goods even under a boom.

Let us take an example of walkman.

Walkman was first introduced by a Japanese company, when and which company I have forgotten.

The first model was to use cassette tape.

Once walkman was introduced by the pioneer company, its competitors followed immediately and the price competition was brought in as usual.

So, the price went down as a natural event of economy.

All this happened during the 1980's when Japan was enjoying its happy boom.

Therefore, we can claim that price cut or whatever you call it does happen even under a boom.

Let us continue the walkman story.

The second type of walkman was introduced by some company (I even don't remember whether its first manufacturer was a Japanese one or not).

In Japan the second model (using MD replacing cassette tape) expelled the first type of walkman very quickly.

Moreover, the price of cassette tape walkman dropped sharply when the second type was introduced and even the price of the second type started to drop once it faced a keen competition with competitors.

This phenomenon also happened during the continuing boom in Japan.

What is interesting is that throughout these events all the manufacturers tried to expel the first type of walkman by themselves by inventing the second better model of walkman out of their own efforts and their hands.

And this competition of invention of new model is still continuing in Japan and we have now the third or fourth type of model which is iPod.

The price of iPod is now as cheap as the second old type or even the old models have already been expelled out of the market by the keen competition of producers by themselves and you can only find them perhaps in the shops selling classical goods!

And if you take a closer look in the manufacturers, what has been happening in all the manufacturers is continuous research, trials and errors of inventing new models everyday and intellectual competitions (regarding electronic technology) are taking place among professionals in the same company or even within the brain and mind of each professional.

And all this intellectual competition causes invention of new models of walkman and this causes price down of the old models and even new models as well regardless under boom or recession.

Therefore, what we can fairly conclude out of this study is that the very cause of deflation (price cut) is intellectual competition among colleagues or rivals or which takes place even within the brain of each oneself.

Therefore, it is a completely false belief that deflation is the cause of recession or you think you can find some country in a deflationary spiral or in a state of deflation.

This phenomenon happens where intellectual competition is keen and it does always happen wherever one single human being is there and it has been deflating all over the world since the beginning of the history as human always wants to contrive some kind of device, tool or machine, and continuously wants to upgrade what others have already invented up until now till he departs this earthly world.

Therefore, we should state that deflation is another name of intellectual competition and improvement which is an intrinsic nature of any human being as far as he is a human.

Therefore, deflationary economy (thus widely believed such as Japan) is only an illusion and it never exists.

Deflation is something that has been there all over the world even under booms and in Japan deflation appears all over the country because demand had fallen short.

And what is the cause of demand?

That is love for others.

Therefore, we can simply conclude that in Japan love for others had decreased or ceased to grow as much as before but intellectual competition, which was hidden beneath the bubble economy but actually had been there since beginning of the history and is and will be active in the country, has come up to the surface of the country because of lack of love for others.

This is the true state of the so called deflationary economy of Japan.

Therefore, we can easily find sad accidents of increasing murders within the family, street killers, suicides in Japan.

Many people are wondering what the cause of the never ending terrible accidents is but the true figure is that we, the Japanese people in general, has lost love for others.

And loss of love for others equals to loss of growing demand and it accelerates deflation (price cut to survive competitions which is getting keener everyday) and recession as well.

But internet and information technology is improving day by day and it naturally nullifies the management of economy based on control of interest rate as we have seen, but the government of Japan has not acquired the future style of management of economy (to be solely run by investment) in its hand yet, thus accelerating the saddening sate of the nation everyday without any solutions.

Coming back to the point, deflation is everywhere where human is there and it never ceases to be there because desire to improve his intellect is an intrinsic nature of human being.

And if we take a closer look at the cause of deflation, as I have just stated above, intellectual improvement or competition is caused by the "desire" to improve intellect of oneself.

Therefore, we should state that deflation is caused by the everlastingly continuing and increasing desire to improve one's intellect.

Inflation is desire to love someone or to live with someone or enlarge oneself in others.

Deflation is desire to improve one's intellect or improve the life on this earthly world.

If you only love yourself, your intellect naturally follows your desire to live happily within your limited self world.

But if you want to love others, your intellect again naturally follows your will and your intellect is used for others and for the common good.

Thus, **love and intellect are always intertwined and growing hand in hand and economy is only a phenomenon reflecting balance of desires of human beings.**

This is the true nature of economy, and inflation and deflation.

Thus, deflation has been fostering civilization throughout the history to improve towards spiritualization or de-materialisation.

We, human beings, have discovered and explored this material earthly world since beginning of the history and all the discoveries, inventions and explorations are owed to the brilliant work of human intellects.

Now that we have already explored the material world, we are going into the age of space and spiritual world.

And all this upgrading of civilization has been always caused by deflation which is the desire to improve human life on this earth intellectually and it naturally leads us to the age of de-materialisation (the age of space and spirit).

In the age of space and spiritual world we need to grasp nature of economy from a different angle as I suppose conventional economics will not catch up entirely with the latest trend of the world and I hope that this book will cast a new light.

PART II. Justice & Love

6) Justice and Love

The biggest philosophical theme which Plato searched throughout his life was "justice".
What is justice?
How justice is to be realized in this earthly world?
How does justice appear in one's soul?
These are the main questions Plato repeatedly asked in his dialogues.

In his masterpiece he attempted to find out what justice is through a dialogue and study it in an imaginary nation, then proceeded to examine it in human soul.
Thus, he started to build a nation in his "Republic".
In "Republic" Socrates (as Plato never appears himself in his dialogues and he made Socrates the main interlocutor) starts to ask;
"A city, I take it, comes into being because each of us is not self-sufficient but needs many things. Can you think any other beginning could found a city?"
"So we each take in different persons for different needs, and needing many things we gather many persons into one dwelling place as partners and helpers, and to this common settlement we give the name of city. Is that correct?"
So, it is division of labour, role or whatever you name it, which inevitably spawns a nation or city in his word.
Then what does happen if you do something you do not know quite well, or somebody else does something he does not know well?

Nation will apparently fall into a state of mismanagement, disorder and even chaos if it goes to an extreme.

Therefore, each one of the citizens must concentrate in his own work, and this is the very basis of the government of a nation.

And justice is found in such a state that the nation is governed harmoniously according to the very fundamental law which is division of labour when every one of the citizens gets the labour suitable to his nature.

Therefore, Socrates (Plato) says,

"What we did lay down and often repeated, if you remember, was that each one must practise that one thing, of all in the city, for which his nature was best fitted.

"Further, that to do one's business and not to meddle with many businesses is justice.

"It seems that really in a sense appears to be justice——to do one's own business."

So, "mind your own business" is justice and not to interfere with others.

This is the definition of the Platonic justice. (The term of the justice we use in our modern world is a bit different form the definition of Platonic justice. And I would like to follow the Platonic meaning of justice in this book.)

Now then, how would you find out and define which work is best fitted for your own nature?

Can anyone carry on the work which he doesn't like?

Can anyone force himself to continue doing something he doesn't like to do?

Or is it not very easy to do something you don't like for many hours without taking a rest?

So, I can fairly claim that something best fitted for your own nature is something you like to do, something you can do no matter how hard it is or some attempt for which you can dare to take any risks to achieve it.

Therefore, the work which is best fitted for your own nature is the work you most like to do, and since justice is, according to Plato, to practise one thing which is best fitted for you, justice is also to do one thing which you most like to do.

By the way, Emanuel Swedenborg, a prodigal genius gifted of a super spiritual ability to visit heaven and hell in the 18th century, said;

"It is very difficult to change your likings in heaven" (for there is no sense of time in the spiritual world and you spend eternal time in a moment).

You spend your time as much as you wish in doing what you like to do in heaven without considering passing of time since there is no time in heaven.

So, you will continue spending your spiritual life in heaven in doing whatever you like to do.

Therefore, heaven is governed harmoniously according to each one's liking.

But this heavenly law is exactly in accordance with what we have just found out.

And if heaven allows us to carry on whatever each one of us likes to pursue without worrying about time, we can also conclude that heaven is full of justice as well.

And heaven is the place where it is full of love of God.

Those who do not believe in the existence of God and love of God can never go back to heaven and those who never love others can also never dwell in heaven.

So, heaven is universally full of love and heaven is the world of love.

Therefore, if you carry on doing whatever you like to do in accordance with your nature without being afraid of taking any risks, it is the very deed of your heavenly love.

Even on the earth each one of us becomes independent by his gifted talent and the talent brings income, love, marriage, family in the end.

So, talent or ability based on one's liking is the basis of love, or we can put it the other way round that **one's love blooms as one's ability or is disguised as one's ability. Therefore, performing one's ability is to perform his love. (And we must not forget that love and intellect always intertwine one another, so, blooming of love also takes blooming of intellect, too, but I am now focusing on the aspect of love.)**

And because justice is to practice what you are best fitted for and that is what you most like to do, and because to do what you like to do is the blooming of your love (and intellect), we can fairly conclude that justice is in fact another name of love that every one of us does his own work which he likes to carry on no matter how hard it is.

Therefore, if we realize the world where each one of us does whatever he likes to do most, we can claim that we have realized the heavenly world.

So, the very pursuance of what you like to do is both justice and love.

And heaven is the world of love and justice where you concentrate on what you are best fitted for.

7) Investment

In our modern world all the governments on the earth are trying to tackle each one of the problems of their nations.

However, most of their efforts are not getting any results.

This is because they are thinking that they can solve the problems somehow by spending so much time, energy and budget.

Problem in general is an accumulation of inability, injustice and vice of human beings. (Natural calamity is also another source of problems but is rather a disaster not a problem.)

And injustice, inability, etc. are all caused by shortcomings, defects, weak points and all kinds of negative elements and aspects of each one of us.

Nobody can ever attain what is not originally talented for himself.

If I am required to overcome my inabilities or defects, for example a simple one such as playing baseball, I will never be able to do it in my life, for I am not a specialist in any sport nor have I a good sense of playing any sports even for fun.

In short it is simply because my soul is not apt for it, I am not made for it and my soul has no liking for it at all.

So, I will never be able to overcome such an inability or defect no matter how much time and money I spend for it.

It is almost impossible to make me do it and if someone (for example my parents) wants me to improve the skill which I lack originally, such an effort will be nullified.

Likewise any government's efforts to tackle accumulating problems will never be successful in solving and overcoming any of them, as far as problems are by themselves gatherings of inabilities of each one of human beings which have been piled up throughout the history of mankind.

Then, how do we solve problems?

It is much faster and easier to develop nations by improving citizens' aptitudes and likings than by tackling a mountain of inabilities of them which definitely end up in wasting so much time, money and energy in vain as every nation has already experienced it over the past many decades and centuries.

In short, improving strong points will naturally wipe out negative aspects either in oneself or in a nation.

And even if he can perform his ability, yet his weak point or disability remains with him.

If every one of any nation performs his best, all the nations will be governed well like heaven and everybody will be busy in performing his best.

So, any nation can create a state where its people can perform their best all the time, though their weaknesses, defects or inabilities still remain within their souls.

But their weak points will never be exhibited to the outer world for they are busy in doing their best.

And this is the very state where heavenly division of labour is attained on this earthly world.

So, every government should immediately take actions to cultivate, improve and develop ability, aptitude, liking of each one of the citizens.

And this is the very mission of politicians (top leaders) of nations to shift the governing rule from tackling the problems (mountains of inabilities) to improving everyone's ability and liking.

Each one of us is given a certain role on this earth and in heaven.

To help every individual to regain his place best fitted for him on this earth is a heavenly mission of politicians.

And to improve everyone's aptitude, ability, liking is the very "justice" and "love" to be performed by politicians of all the nations.

Now then, what can be actual policy to be implemented by governments of all the nations to improve each individual's aptitude and ability?
That is best realized by "investment".
Direct investment by government to each individual to improve his aptitude, or company's hopeful technology, new project together with job training, mental education towards self-reliance is the very policy which government should take to stimulate economy and upgrade the life standard of the people.
We should not misjudge that poverty in itself is problem.
In fact not being given of any chance to improve one's aptitude and to perform his talent is the very misery for each one of us.
Therefore, giving only money to those in poverty without providing any chance to perform their aptitude, ability or to challenge their dream always fails.

8) Summary
Let us combine all the philosophical discoveries in this book.

As we have examined, management of economy by controlling interest rate will be soon nullified because information technology (statistics technology) is improving rapidly everyday and it will put an end to the deed of money-lending which was generated out of lack of statistics technology or slow transactions of statistic figure of nations.
(Interest is merely transfer of money in the community and never

creates wealth by itself anyway. It is imperative to print or mint money if any government wishes to increase the wealth and the quantity of money that circulates and accumulates in the nation, for printing and minting money alone increases the quantity of money.)

Therefore, when the deed of money-lending has ceased, economy will be solely managed by investment which encourages and fosters each one of us to improve our talents, aptitudes, likings and abilities.

And liking is the very love of oneself.

And improving liking (love) is resulted in increase of population (increase of demand) and intellect as well.

Therefore, investment in each one's liking, aptitude, ability will increase entire demand of a nation as a result and the nation (the central government not the central bank) can print or mint more money (crystalisation of love and intellect) which is to circulate in the nation.

And it is easy to grasp that profit of any enterprise or business is merely the fruit of one's love and intellect which one has added to the community which one belongs to.

The love and intellect you added to this world returns to you as money (crystalisation of love and intellect).

Furthermore, the country which is facing a high inflation can take policies to increase intellect of each one of its citizens which fosters deflationary effect on the economy and it will lead to curb the prices of goods in general by improving productivity of the offices and factories nationwide.

On the other hand when a nation is suffering from serious deflation like Japan, which implies that love for others is decreasing or not growing in the country, the central government or leaders of the nation can take policies to nourish love among the families of the nation.

But we must study carefully what kind of remedies can be taken for the recovery from the deflation in such a country as Japan where the people are facing a heavy loss of love. (But this is a very rare case.)

This is how Platonic justice, that is to encourage and help everyone to improve his liking and aptitude which is the fruit of his love and intellect in short, is to be attained on this earthly world, and that is the very mission and love of politician as well.

PART III. Practise in Nepal

9) Nepal

I received the first contact from Nepal at the end of August in 2008 when I had lessons of Japanese language to foreigners.

I posted a free advertisement of my lessons on the internet and Mr. Rameswar Dhamala found my advertisement and contacted me by e-mail.

His main purpose of the contact was to ask me to help the development of Nepal somehow. He had been looking for someone who can help him to develop the country.

But I didn't have any idea of dealing with him anyway, so, I kept trying to refuse his offers during the first few months. However, he was "obstinate" in asking me to help him any way possible to me.

So, we kept communicating through e-mails almost everyday and many ideas came up and disappeared by the end of 2008.

He came to Tokyo at the end of the year and we met for the first time in Tokyo on the January 1st and I introduced him to an owner of agriculture farm who offered acceptance of some agriculture trainees from Nepal to train them in his farm. He had accepted over some thousands of trainees from Asian countries over the past years.

Since then we started working together to take permission from the Nepali government to dispatch Nepali agriculture trainees to Japan but finally the owner of the agriculture farm got into trouble last year and the project has been suspended till now.

However, this was only a beginning to establish our mutual trust and long term relationship.

One night I had a dream in the middle of September 2010 and heard a heavenly voice in the dream asking me;
"Why don't you go to Nepal?!"
So, I took the flight to Nepal once again (this was my second visit) on the 12th October last year. (This kind of spiritual phenomenon happens to me often.)

10) The Project in Khalchet village, Sangkosh, Dhading, Nepal

After some research in Nepal with Rameswar I finally decided to invest a tiny sum of money in the village where Mr. Rameswar Dhamala is from and his family lives in.
The village is a beautiful farming village with lots of paddy fields in a mountainous area which is in the district just west next to Kathmandu.
It takes about three hours by express taxi from Kathmandu to the capital of the district and it still takes about two hours by trekking from there.
I told him that I would invest 40,000 Nepali Rupees to buy seeds of vegetable for the farmers to plant in the village.
The population of the village is about four hundred (about 70 households) and upon my offer to invest they summoned a whole village meeting to discuss how to utilize my money.
What they decided was to divide the whole farming areas of the village into four big areas and each area to be divided into ten to twelve small parts in which everybody of the village cultivates and enjoys the harvest.
There are two big families in the village and they agreed to provide a large area of their farming land to those who do not have their own farming land.

The villagers agreed to set up and officially register an agriculture co-operative body to foster this project, which is, according to the Ministry of Agriculture, still very few in Nepal, though anybody can register and start agriculture co-operative by law. (The body registered was named Manarupi Agriculture Co-operative, Ltd.)

Though the procedure took some time, the project started smoothly and they planted the seeds of potato, radish, cabbage, carrot, etc.

In the beginning I experienced an argument about how to start the project with my partner who was saying or the farmers were saying through him as they don't speak English and I don't speak their language that they would be able to get more harvest if they had modern plough machine, if they had greenhouse to raise vegetable, if they had a four ton truck, if they had chemically improved fertiliser and this kind of many if, if, if…

So, I told my partner;

"You must fight with what you have right now. Then others will come to help you.

For example, Japan is now a developed country but we were like Nepal about one hundred and forty years ago when we started a national revolutionary effort to catch up the western civilization (in 1867).

So, just forget and give up dreaming of what you do not have at the moment.

You have to start fighting with what you are gifted of now.

You have rich rewarding nature, buffalos for milking and ploughing, irrigation systems all over the village though very simple, you can start planting vegetable right now.

So, you must start it immediately without dreaming.

The more you become self reliant without dreaming of what you do not have at the moment, the more helps from others will come." Such an argument and persuasion continued for some time but I pushed them to start buying seeds and planting them. I believe this is a kind of mental education towards self-reliance.

Therefore, investment should come hand in hand with education (cause of deflation) and education towards self reliance is not always found in the school textbooks.

It is the mental and spiritual education of how to be self-reliant for the Nepali farmers and this is one of the very essences and purposes of the project.

(On the other hand if I would invest in Japan, I must provide Japanese with mental education and training to regain and improve love for others (cause of inflation) along with investment.)

Anyway, they planted so many potato, cabbage and other seeds in their land by the time I left Nepal on the 17th in November last year and they are getting an unexpectedly huge volume of vegetable (total of 21,340 kilogrammes mostly potato). The villagers of Khalchet were also surprised themselves at an enormous volume.

(I named this small amount investment "microinvestment" that encourages villages and can produce so much products and rewards in return.)

I visited once again this village in April this year and visited some houses of the farmers of the village with Rameswar and found in every house four hundred to eight hundred kilogrammes of potato stored in the second floor of their houses (second floor is usually the storage room of vegetable in the village (maybe so all over the country).

It was a big surprise to me that rich nature has rewarded so much to their toils!

So, we had another happy problem which is to sell out the vegetable!

I and Rameswar spent many days to think of how to deliver the vegetable and to where.

Finally Rameswar was inspired of an idea to sell the vegetable in Kathmandu market off season when the price of potato is higher throughout a year.

The Khalchet village had the stock of about 15,000 kilogrammes of vegetable during my visit and it is impossible to sell out such a huge volume of vegetable in the nearest market which has the population of only 8,000 people who live in the capital of the district. And that is the only market closest to the village and they need to trek and carry down for one and a half hours to the market.

However, the villagers have to sell the vegetable anyway, so, they also started by the end of April to sell in the market of the capital of the district which is called Dhading Besi using a small carrier.

11) A Policy Proposal to the Nepali Government

Here is a concern regarding the management of the nation's economy.

According to the statistics of Nepal, the population of the country has been growing over the years, which means that the overall demand of the nation has also been growing.

And there is not any statistics showing unemployment rate of the nation but I found on the internet an estimated unemployment rate which is 43%.

However, this is only an estimate and is on the internet, so, it is not completely trustable.

But even if the figure is true, I do have a different impact about the definition of unemployment in the case of Nepal.

I take that the word "unemployment" usually means that someone has lost his job who had a job before and has a motivation to work. Whereas in Nepal I have found in Khalchet village for example many people are working to get food and milk for everyday life. Water is flowing out anywhere in the village as the mountain is rich in unpolluted pure water and there is no problem in irrigation at all, though it is very simple.

And each member of the Rameswar's family is very hard working, almost working from early morning till evening but they never spend even a penny of money.

It means that they are not dependent on money in the village as much as my country is.

So, they are not poor but they don't need money in the village. And they are perhaps classified as "jobless" if we follow the standard of the developed countries for they never earn money. But in fact they are as hard working as the people of the developed countries.

The family sometimes sells rice in the market and of course they use money once they are out of the village.

Furthermore, there are many people who are starving and dying out of poverty in the far side of the country where I have not visited yet.

(Just to grasp the nation's true figure…Rameswar's family sometimes has guests who, according to the family, are poor in the village and have no farming land of their own and they are visiting round richer families everyday to get food.

Surprisingly the family serves dishes to them and even gives them some souvenir (usually fruits or snacks) naturally and automatically like a conditioned reflex when the visitors appear without considering so much about their custom. I didn't see many of these visitors but a certain number of dwellers are wandering through the village everyday for survival and in the village next to Khalchet there are also some wanderers. According to Rameswar my partner, there are wandering this kind of people in the country.)

Considering all these experiences, my general impression is that there is not enough money circulating in the nation.
And the people are in general unemployed and jobless according to the standard of developed nations but they are very hard working which contradicts against the entire sense of the developed countries.
And according to the Ministry of Agriculture and Co-Operative, Nepal imports so much vegetables and fruits from India and China.
In fact you can find apples and cabbages from China, grapes from India, and such and such in anywhere in Kathmandu.
But actually the nature of Khalchet is very rich, rewarding and always ready to produce vegetable and fruit for the people who industriously invest their farming efforts.
So, what I can derive out of these facts and experiences are;
1. Nepal government can print more money and pump it in every village all over the country. Inflation is creeping up in Kathmandu but there is so much shortage of money in rural villages, and thus villagers are living without money. Many young people have to leave the country to earn money. But foreign currency is to be exchanged when they come back to the country and it further drives the shortage of Nepali Rupees and causes inflation in the country, if the government does not print more money (Rupees). If I may exaggerate the situation of Nepal, we can imagine that a half of the country

is working and the other half is resting, and the money has been circulating among the half of the working people so far, and now the other half has stood up and stopped resting and started to work and they need money for living. What the government has to do now is to print enough money for the people who has just stood up and joined the other half who are working, otherwise the nation's economy will not be able to take off.
2. When the Government pumps money, the Government has to guide every village to use the invested money for agriculture or whatever enterprise the people wish to do for their living. In other words, the Government has to provide money and job consultation or training simultaneously, otherwise it only causes inflation and it won't foster the industriousness amongst the nationals.
3. Mental education must be provided for the people to encourage them to "fight with what they have". This is a very simple but ultimate rule to master when the country wants to develop its economy. If the people wish to make too big a leap from the present situation, they won't be able to grow. In the case of Khalchet village, they had to start with the technology they have at the moment which is to plough with buffalos, to plant seeds without greenhouses, fertilizer is the buffalos' dung, etc. Therefore, I urged my partner and the villagers to fight with what they have. Result has already been brought in and more helps are now coming in the village, because they are continuously making efforts and completely stopped daydreaming of acquiring what they do not have at the moment. And this ultimate rule (to fight with what you have) is the most important and shortest

way towards development, and this rule makes people more industrious, self-reliant and united among themselves.

Anyway, what they are tested now is to have courage to print their own money and invest in each one's dream and challenge of their citizens. That is the very mission of the Government.

12) Foreign Currency

I and Rameswar often have meaningful arguments and exchange opinions over the management of economy, politics, civilization in general, etc. And the last one we had was about foreign currency.

One of the worldwide beliefs that I suppose the developing countries might have is that they are trying hard to obtain more foreign strong currencies like US dollars, Euro and Japanese Yen and they tend to believe that acquiring foreign currencies can increase the economic power of the nation.

It is true that they can import more goods from overseas by the reserves of the acquired foreign currencies.

However, it is also true that any foreign currency never circulates and be used as national currency for daily use in any foreign country (except when a country accepts it as its national currency), and importation of foreign goods using the reserves of the foreign currencies does never increase the power of the nation, if the people of the country never try to improve their life by themselves. Importing goods from overseas without industriousness improved within only makes the country dependent on foreign countries.

So, what developing nations have to do is to encourage the people's industriousness by printing money and to invest money into each one of their businesses, projects, enterprises or challenges with job training, mental education and management consultation, thus increase step by step the quantity of the money that circulates in the nation and strengthen the nation's currency by motivating the industriousness within, for the power of any currency is entirely based upon the strength of love (often interpreted as the spirit of self-reliance) and intellect of the people.

We must not forget that currency is money and money is the crystalisaton of love and intellect of the people.

Therefore, exchange of currencies is exchange of love and intellect, and if a nation depends on the foreign currencies, it means the nation is dependent on the love and intellect of the foreign countries. And investment from foreign countries has the same effect upon the economy of the country.

Therefore, any governments of developing nations must go on their own ways to develop their countries by printing and pumping their own currency step by step (which equals to the increment of their own love and intellect) and thus the exchange rate against foreign currencies will naturally improve along with their daily efforts which purpose is to depart from the dependence on foreign countries.

Epilogue

Each human being consists of love for others and love for oneself. It is only a matter of balance of both kinds of love that varies economy of each individual and each family.

And every nation consists of millions of humans who are living to love others and themselves and its economy fluctuates in accordance with their love.

So does the world.

Therefore, the world is simply a creation of the balance between love for others and love for oneself.

Intellect and knowledge improves along with love (both for others and oneself).

Economy is merely a materialized phenomenon in which love and intellect disguise themselves as money (or wealth).

So, why do we have to make it difficult to understand its nature by complicating it with mathematics. macro-economics, micro-economics and all that?

Human civilization started from scratch without any modern technology and it inevitably spawned money-lenders who never create wealth.

However, we have got the technology which will make such a deed totally nullified in the coming future, which is a natural result of human history.

It seems that human progress has come back to the beginning point where we started in which we had enjoyed pure life where humans could perform their own best (love).

It is just like we have gone through one big circle of progress in a few thousand years and we have come back to the starting point after so many bitter experiences and lessons and we have to start again from the original query of how love blooms in every field of human activity in this world to attain a higher realm of understanding and enlightenment.

After more than twenty years of philosophical quest, **it has become quite clear to me that economy is only a reflection of love and intellect.**
Therefore, management of economy of a nation entirely depends on improving love and intellect, which needs a balance.
And inflation is caused by the desire to love someone or to live with someone or enlarge oneself in others.
Deflation is caused by the desire to improve one's intellect or improve the life on this earthly world.
Therefore, balance of love and intellect is the balance of desires (love and intellect) of one's soul. And these desires generated money in the course of history.
So, management of the balance of love and intellect (management of desires of one's soul) is the management of economy of a nation and even of a family, a single human being.

Investment by government to foster ability, aptness, liking of each one of citizens will be more important after the deed of money lending is nullified in the coming future, for love blooms out of one's ability.
And love and intellect grow hand in hand. So, investment in one's ability equals to investment in one's love and intellect.
Therefore, stimulation of economy by investment is equal to

encouraging or nourishing love and intellect of citizens, and it will be very important for economists to know how love develops itself in the soul of each oneself, in a family and in a nation and to master how love and intellect have been, are and will be intertwined and improved in this earthly world throughout the entire history of mankind.

Therefore, we can fairly claim that economics is now transformed into philosophical analysis of love and intellect and we even need a help of spiritualism which is bourgeoning all over the world now and casting a new light upon the love and intellect of a higher realm. This fosters unification of every field of academy.

So, economics should be upgraded to catch up with such a unifying trend of the world and it needs to be illumined with a new philosophical light, too.

May 16, 2011

Nakayama, Kunitaka

Thank you for reading my book.
Your comments and feedbacks are most welcome.
Please do not hesitate to contact me.

Contacts of the Author:
___

Nakayama, Kunitaka
Tokyo Fuchu-shi Oshitate-machi 1-35-71-305, Japan
House phone : 0423-60-8031 (from overseas 81-423-60-8031)
Mobile phone : 090-5788-5682 (from overseas 81-90-5788-5682)
E-mail : kunitaka@a01.itscom.net
URL : http://www.akademeia.ne.jp

www.ingramcontent.com/pod-product-compliance
Lightning Source LLC
Chambersburg PA
CBHW061515040426
42450CB00008B/1628